Amazing Paint!

Becca Heddle

OXFORD
UNIVERSITY PRESS

OXFORD
UNIVERSITY PRESS

Great Clarendon Street, Oxford OX2 6DP

Oxford University Press is a department of the University of Oxford.
It furthers the University's objective of excellence in research, scholarship,
and education by publishing worldwide in

Oxford   New York

Auckland   Cape Town   Dar es Salaam   Hong Kong   Karachi
Kuala Lumpur   Madrid   Melbourne   Mexico City   Nairobi
New Delhi   Shanghai   Taipei   Toronto

With offices in

Argentina   Austria   Brazil   Chile   Czech Republic   France   Greece
Guatemala   Hungary   Italy   Japan   Poland   Portugal   Singapore
South Korea   Switzerland   Thailand   Turkey   Ukraine   Vietnam

Oxford is a registered trade mark of Oxford University Press
in the UK and in certain other countries

British Library Cataloguing in Publication Data

Data available

ISBN 978-0-19-919844-3

7   9   10   8

Printed in China by Imago

Paper used in the production of this book is a natural,
recyclable product made from wood grown in sustainable forests.
The manufacturing process conforms to the environmental
regulations of the country of origin.

Acknowledgements

The publisher would like to thank the following for permission to reproduce photographs: p4cl Gianni Dagli Orti/Corbis UK Ltd., p4bl Charles & Josette Lenars/Corbis UK Ltd., p4cc Roger De La Harpe/Gallo Images/Corbis UK Ltd., p4bc&4/5t&b National Gallery Collection; By kind permission of the Trustees of the National Gallery, London/Corbis UK Ltd., p4cr Archivo Iconografico, S.A./Corbis UK Ltd.; p5cl Francis G. Mayer/Corbis UK Ltd., p5bl The Barnes Foundation, Merion Station, Pennsylvania/Corbis UK Ltd., p5bc Burstein Collection/Corbis UK Ltd., p5cr Martha Holmes/Time Life Pictures/Getty Images, p5br Scala Art Resource, p5tr Bridgeman Art Library; p6c Gianni Dagli Orti/Corbis UK Ltd., p6b Roger De La Harpe/Gallo Images/Corbis UK Ltd., p6/7t Charles & Josette Lenars/Corbis UK Ltd.; p7b Pierre Vauthey/Sygma/Corbis UK Ltd.; p8l Josè Manuel Sanchis Calvete/Corbis UK Ltd., p8r Archivo Iconografico, S.A./Corbis UK Ltd.; p9l National Gallery Collection; By kind permission of the Trustees of the National Gallery, London/Corbis UK Ltd., p9r Jacqui Hurst/Corbis UK Ltd.; p10l Josè Manuel Sanchis Calvete/Corbis UK Ltd., p10r National Gallery Collection; By kind permission of the Trustees of the National Gallery, London/Corbis UK Ltd.; p11 National Gallery Collection; By kind permission of the Trustees of the National Gallery, London/Corbis UK Ltd.; p14r National Gallery Collection; By kind permission of the Trustees of the National Gallery, London/Corbis UK Ltd.; p15l Christopher Cormack/Corbis UK Ltd., p15r Jacqui Hurst/Corbis UK Ltd.; p16t James Marshall/Corbis UK Ltd., p16c Jacques M. Chenet/Corbis UK Ltd., p16b Hubert Stadler/Corbis UK Ltd.; p17 Martha Holmes/Time Life Pictures/Getty Images; p18b National Gallery Collection; By kind permission of the Trustees of the National Gallery, London/Corbis UK Ltd.; p19tl&tr The Barnes Foundation, Merion Station, Pennsylvania/Corbis UK Ltd., p19b Francis G. Mayer/Corbis UK Ltd.; p20t Bridgeman Art Library; p20b Scala Art Resource; p21t Scala Art Resource, p21b Bridgeman Art Library; p22t Bettmann/Corbis UK Ltd., p22b Bridgeman Art Library; p23t Kevin Weaver/Hulton/Getty Images, p23b Burstein Collection/Corbis UK Ltd.

Cover photo: Alamy

Additional photography by MM Studios

Illustrations by David Mostyn

Contents

A lot of painters have names which are hard to say. If a name is shown *like this* you can find out how to say it on page 24.

Always painting

People have painted throughout our entire history. We use everything we possibly can to paint with or on. The timeline below shows you when the pictures you will see in this book were made. But just think – the pictures in this book are only a tiny fraction of the ones that exist all over the world.

15

80,000 years ago
Altamira cave
paintings, Spain

8,000 years ago
bushman cave
paintings, Africa

1304

1276–1337
Giotto, Italy

16–40,000
years ago
Australian cave
paintings

c.23,000 BC

600–1000 years ago
the Middle Ages

1410–1420

1881–1973
Picasso, Spain

1937

1485–1576
Titian, Italy

1912–1956
Pollock, USA

1949

1853–1890
Van Gogh, Holland

1888

1903–1970
Rothko, USA

1863–1944
Munch, Norway

1390–1441
Van Eyck, Holland

1859–1891
Seurat, France

1893

1949

1885

5

Really old paint

The oldest paintings are in caves and on rocks. There are lots in Europe, Africa and Australia.

People painted these animals in a Spanish cave thousands of years ago. They used chalk, coloured earth and **charcoal** to make the paintings.

A five-year-old girl found the pictures in 1879 when she was exploring the cave with her father.

Although these pictures in Australia are very old, they are still important to the tribes they belong to.

How have they lasted so long?

The paintings are out of the sun, rain and wind so they have kept really well. But light – and even visitors' breath – can harm the pictures. At Lascaux in France, they have made a copy of the pictures for visitors, to help save the real ones.

Really expensive paint

By the **Middle Ages**, painters had discovered many more colours, though some cost a lot. The best, strongest colours came from stones that were used in jewellery. The stones were valuable in themselves, and the time taken to make them into paint made the colours very expensive.

This stone, lapis lazuli, was ground up to make a blue called ultramarine. It took days of hard work to make the colour. Imagine how much it cost to do this ceiling by Giotto!

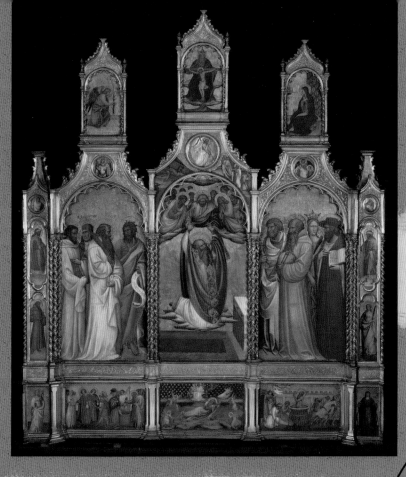

The red called vermilion cost as much as gold.

Artists even used real gold – coins hammered out until they were thinner than paper. They stuck down the gold and rubbed it to make it smooth and shiny. Some people said you had to rub it with a wild bear's tooth!

Really dangerous paint

Have you ever thought that paint could be dangerous? Some paints could even kill you!

Poison yellow

Many of the colours old artists used were poisonous. This yellow, called orpiment, is actually the deadly poison arsenic. You had to be very careful not to suck your paintbrush!

Goblin blue

The stone that gives this blue, called cobalt, was dug out of caves in Germany. If the miners got their skin wet, the stone could eat away at the skin, causing terrible injuries. The German word for a goblin is kobold – say 'cob-olt' – just like the colour. It is the perfect name for something nasty that lives in a cave and might harm you!

Some paints that artists use today are still poisonous, but children cannot buy them.

11

All change!

You know you can make new colours by mixing: blue and yellow make green, for example. But colours can change for more mysterious reasons too. Try these experiments to see what can happen.

Chemical changes

You need:

red cabbage
saucepan
water
three glasses
lemon juice
bicarbonate of soda

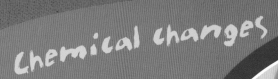

Get an adult to help you boil up some red cabbage in water.

Then strain off the water and keep it. It should be purple, like the cabbage.

Put some cabbage water in each of three glasses. Add lemon juice to one and bicarbonate to another. Leave the third one plain.

The cabbage water changes colour! Lemon juice turns it pink. Bicarbonate turns it blue-green.

Some paint colours can change in the same way, when the **chemicals** in them **react** together.

Changes over time

You need:

lemon juice
paper
cotton bud or
cocktail stick

Draw a face with lemon juice. It's invisible!

Keep the paper a few days – put it in a warm place to speed things up.

The picture changes colour so you can see it.

Paint colours can change over time too – these leaves were originally green.

Paint made from what?

You probably use watercolours, and know about oil paint – but people have made paint from all sorts of other things.

Cave painters mostly used animal fat from their food, or glue made by boiling up animal skins and bones.

Painters in the Middle Ages used egg yolk to make a paint called tempera. It was like painting with mayonnaise! But the colours stayed bright and lasted well.

Slapping it on

When you think of painting, you probably think of brushes. But artists using oil paint can use a kind of knife too – and there are lots of other ways of putting paint on a picture.

The oldest ways

Many painters, including cave men, painted in the same way you probably first did – using fingers. The famous Italian painter Titian used his fingers as much as his brush.

To make these hand prints, the cave men probably blew paint out of their mouths. It was a good thing that it wasn't poisonous!

A modern way

'Action painters' like Jackson Pollock did use a brush – but they didn't put it on the canvas. They laid the canvas on the floor and splattered paint on it from above. Pollock even used a bicycle on some of his pictures.

The colours we see

Find a piece of cloth that is one plain colour – maybe a T-shirt or a towel. Look really carefully – does it really all look the same colour?

There are shadows in folds and crinkles, and lighter patches where the fabric stands up or light hits it differently. It adds up to lots of different colours. But how can you show this in a painting?

Some artists put on paint in layers: Van Eyck did this, using see-through paint on top of solid paint.

Artists like **Seurat** used lots of tiny dots of different colours. This is called pointillism. It gives a sort of shimmery effect.

Some artists choose colours that show how they feel, rather than how things actually look. **Van Gogh** used weird colour combinations to show his emotions.

How big?

A painting can be just about any size. It depends on the artist, where the picture is for, how it is made and what its purpose is.

Tiny paintings

Hundreds of years ago, before there were photos, wealthy people used to carry round tiny paintings called miniatures. It was a bit like having a photo in your wallet or purse.

Wall paintings

These **frescoes** cover the whole wall of the church they are in: in fact, they are part of it! Frescoes are painted when the plaster on the wall is still wet, so they last as long as the walls themselves.

Huge paintings

Some paintings are big because that looks best. This colour painting is over two metres tall.

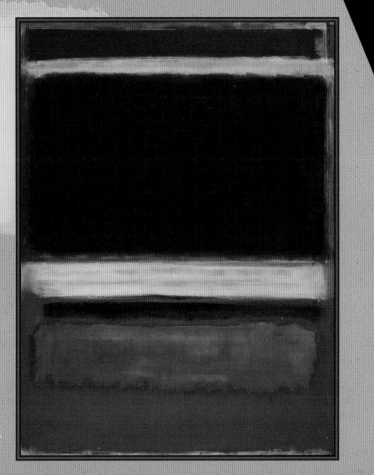

Picasso made this painting called **Guernica** enormous because he was so angry about the bombing it shows.

What's it for?

Paint is amazing in so many ways. But why do we paint?

Many paintings show people's religious beliefs or other ideas. Early peoples painted in secret places, such as in caves.

Frescoes show bible stories in a sort of cartoon strip – for people who couldn't read.

NEW YORK WELCOMES
ELSON MANDELA & THE ANC
KEEP THE PRESSURE ON APARTHEID

People paint their political beliefs too: for example, huge **murals** all over the world show Nelson Mandela, the first black president of South Africa.

Many painters want to capture what they see: portraits record a person, time and place. Other pictures like Munch's The Scream record a strong feeling.

Other paintings are just for the joy of colour, or to show what the artist can do. Next time you look at paintings, ask yourself why and how they were made – it makes them all the more amazing!

Index

Glossary

charcoal – burnt wood that can be used for drawing

chemicals – the substances that something is made up of

fresco – a kind of painting which covers a whole wall, and was done when the plaster was wet

Middle Ages a time in history from about AD1100–1400

mural – a very large painting, done straight onto a wall

react – when chemicals have an effect on each other and change because of it, this is called a reaction

Pronunciation guide

Giotto: Jot–oh

Guernica: Gurr–nicker

Lascaux: Lass–co

Munch: Munk

Seurat: Ser–at (but try not to say the t)

tempera: temper–er

Titian: Tish–un

Van Eyck: Van Ike

Van Gogh: Van Goff